WONDERS
OF THE WORLD

WONDERS OF THE WORLD

Awe-inspiring places from around the world

amber
BOOKS

First published in 2019

Published by
Amber Books Ltd
United House
North Road
London
N7 9DP
United Kingdom
www.amberbooks.co.uk
Instagram: www.instagram.com/amberbooksltd
Facebook: www.facebook.com/amberbooks
Twitter: @amberbooks

ISBN: 978-1-78274-776-5

Project Editor: Sarah Uttridge
Designer: Hart McLeod
Picture Research: Terry Forshaw

Printed in China

Contents

Introduction

Many lists of the wonders of the world have been compiled since the ancient Greek historian Herodotus (c. 484–425 BC) is said to have put together his list of seven wonders, only one of which survives – the Pyramid of Khufu at Giza. Contemporary lists of wonders include technological achievements such as the World Wide Web and natural features that are in desperate need of our protection, such as the polar ice caps and Amazon rainforest. Whether they are natural or manmade, all the wonders ever listed have one thing in common: they fill us with awe. That may be awe at the beauty of the natural world, the extraordinary power of the physical forces that shape our planet or the apparent ingenuity of evolution. Alternatively, it may be awe at the splendour of man-made monuments, the devotion of their craftspeople or the sheer ambition of rulers and architects who aimed to build taller, wider, longer and more innovatively than ever before. From the temples of ancient civilizations to the skyscrapers of today, from the deserts of Iran to the Great Barrier Reef, we can only wonder at our planet's many treasures.

ABOVE:
Adélie penguins live only on the coasts of Antarctica, making them one of the most southerly bird species.
RIGHT:
Antarctica, the last continent to be reached by humans, is the world's largest desert.

Africa and the Middle East

The Middle East, at the crossroads between Eurasia and Africa, has for millennia been a region where natural riches and trade have spurred on great advances and new ideas. The region was the cradle of the world's earliest civilizations, in Mesopotamia and Egypt. It was also the birthplace of the world religions Judaism, Christianity and Islam. Helped by stocks of crude oil, the region remains at the centre of world affairs today, both spiritually, politically and economically, a fact testified to by wonders such as the site of the world's largest pilgrimage, the Great Mosque of Mecca; the tallest building, the Burj Khalifa; and the largest manmade island, Palm Jumeirah.

The Middle East spread its influence across North Africa and beyond, as can be seen by the African continent's monumental mosques and churches, as well as the neglected pyramids of Sudan. Yet Africa has countless wonders unique to itself, testament to its home-grown ideas and beauties, from the ancient stone city of Great Zimbabwe to the powerful Victoria Falls. Some of Africa's greatest natural wonders are in need of our protection, including the critically endangered mountain gorillas of the Central African cloud forests. Today, numerous national parks draw travellers and protect the continent's extraordinary flora and fauna, from the wetlands of the Okavango Delta to the shrubland of South Africa.

OPPOSITE:
Pyramids, Giza, Egypt
The three main pyramids at Giza were tombs for the Fourth Dynasty pharaohs (from left to right) Khufu (c. 2589–2566 BC), Khafre (c. 2558–2532 BC) and Menkaure (c. 2532–2503 BC). At 146.5m (481ft) high, the pyramid of Khufu is the largest of the three and was the world's tallest manmade structure for more than 3800 years.

Great Sphinx of Giza, Egypt
Around 73m (240ft) long, the
Sphinx depicts a mythical
creature with the body of
a lion and the head of a
human, believed to represent
the face of Pharaoh Khafre,
whose pyramid lies about
500m (1600ft) due west.
This guardian statue, carved
directly into the limestone
bedrock of the Giza plateau,
was probably intended
to show the ruler's close
relationship with the sun
deity Sekhmet, a lioness.

ABOVE:

Aswan Dam, Egypt

Completed in 1970, this dam across the Nile in southern Egypt was built to regulate the river's seasonal flooding, store water for irrigation and generate hydroelectric power. The dam created Lake Nasser, named after Gamal Abdel Nasser, the second president of Egypt. At 5250 sq km (2030 sq miles), Nasser is one of the largest man-made lakes in the world and stretches over the border into northern Sudan, where it takes the name Lake Nubia.

OPPOSITE:

Dead Sea, Jordan, Israel and Palestine

The surface of this hypersaline lake is 430.5m (1412ft) below sea level, making it the lowest elevation on Earth's land. The water is 9.6 times saltier than the ocean, creating an environment in which most animals and plants cannot live and so earning the lake its name. The salts (sodium chloride, magnesium chloride, calcium chloride and others) make the water so dense that it is famously easy for swimmers to float.

Dome of the Rock, Jerusalem

This Islamic shrine is located on Temple Mount in Jerusalem, a city holy to Muslims, Jews and Christians. For Muslims, this site is sacred for the rock at the building's centre, which was the starting point for the Prophet Muhammad's Night Journey, both a physical and spiritual journey taken around 621 AD. The octagonal building was initially completed in 691, with the current dome built in 1023 and the exterior tilework added by the Ottomans in the 16th century.

LEFT:
Burj Khalifa, Dubai, United Arab Emirates
Since 2008, this skyscraper has been the world's tallest building, with a height of 829.8m (2722ft). Designed by Adrian Smith of Skidmore, Owings & Merrill, the firm that also designed One World Trade Center in New York, the building echoes the Islamic architecture of the region, in particular the spiralling shape of the minaret of the 9th-century Great Mosque of Samarra, in Iraq.

ABOVE:
125th Floor Observation Deck, Burj Khalifa
At 456m (1496ft) above the ground, the 125th-floor observation deck offers dizzying views over the city and the Persian Gulf. Offsetting its sleek glass and metal, the deck's designers used a carved wooden ceiling to evoke a traditional Arabic *mashrabiya*, the projecting upper-storey window surrounded by latticework found in homes from the Middle Ages to the mid-20th century.

Palm Jumeirah, Dubai, United Arab Emirates

Work on the construction of the world's largest artificial island began in 2001 and lasted six years. Palm Jumeirah is in the shape of a palm tree, with a surrounding crescent-shaped island that acts as a breakwater. The development, which is connected to the mainland by monorail, hosts 28 hotels and 4500 residential properties.

FAR LEFT:

Al-Balad, Jeddah, Saudi Arabia

The old city of Jeddah, known as Al-Balad ('The Town'), was founded in the 7th century. It preserves a Red Sea architectural tradition, with many tower houses built of coral stone and teak, decorated by traditional wooden window screens called *roshan*.

LEFT:

Great Mosque, Mecca, Saudi Arabia

The largest mosque in the world, the Great Mosque surrounds the Kaaba ('The Cube'), the most sacred site of Islam. The Quran states that the Kaaba's foundations were laid by Abraham and Ishmael. All over the world, Muslims face the Kaaba when praying. During the yearly Hajj, about 1.8 million pilgrims circle the building, which is considered the Bayt Allah ('House of God').

Al-Khazneh, Petra

Al-Khazneh ('The Treasury')
was actually built as a
mausoleum for the Nabatean
king Aretas IV (c. 9 BC–AD
40). Although the exterior
statues have been much eroded
by wind and rain, we can
still see mythological figures
connected with the afterlife,
including four eagles to carry
away the souls of the dead.

Petra, Jordan

The city of Petra, in the
desert of southern Jordan,
was carved from sandstone
cliffs about 2000 years ago by
the Nabateans. At its peak,
the city was a major trading
hub, at the centre of several
overland trade routes, and
home to 20,000 people.

LEFT:

Medina of Sousse

The maze-like medina (from the Arabic for 'old city') of Sousse was declared a UNESCO world heritage site in 1988, as a perfect example of a walled town dating from the early centuries of Islam. The winding, blind-alley streets were a defence against the pirates that often attacked this coastal city.

FAR LEFT:

Great Mosque, Sousse, Tunisia

Completed in AD 851, the Great Mosque has no minaret, so the call to prayer is made from the domed kiosk (pictured here) in the northeast corner of the *sahn*, or courtyard. The mosque's architect adapted an earlier fort, which explains the crenellated exterior wall.

Nubian pyramids, Meroë, Sudan
More than 350 pyramids were built as tombs for the kings and queens of the Kushite kingdoms of
Napata and Meroë. These wealthy trading and metal-working kingdoms of the Nile Valley, which
thrived between the 8th century BC and 4th century AD, were influenced by the culture of nearby
Egypt. Nubian pyramids are usually between 6 and 30m (20 and 98ft) tall, with bases no more
than 8m (26ft) wide, making their sides much more steeply sloping than Egyptian pyramids.

Pyramid entrance, Meroë
Many of the Meroë pyramids had H-shaped entrances at their bases, leading into offering temples decorated with wall paintings. Most of the pyramid tombs, which once contained the occupant's mummified remains and sarcophagus as well as jewellery, furniture, pottery and other precious objects, were plundered many centuries ago. The pyramids faced further disaster when many had their tops blown off by the 19th-century Italian treasure-hunter Giuseppe Ferlini.

**Erg Chebbi,
Sahara Desert, Morocco**
Ergs, or sand seas, are known
for their shifting dunes. The
dunes of Erg Chebbi, which
rise to a height of 150m
(492ft), are at the far northern
borders of the Sahara Desert.
With an area of 9,200,000
sq km (3,600,000 sq miles),
stretching over much of North
Africa, the Sahara is the
world's largest hot desert.

Okavango Delta, Botswana
This swampy inland delta of the Okavango River does not flow into any sea. All the water, which pools in a tectonic trough, eventually evaporates or is consumed by transpiration by plants. The most populous large mammal here is the red lechwe (pictured), a species of antelope with splayed hooves, long hind legs and a greasy, water-repellent coat, which enable it to move quickly through knee-deep water.

LEFT:
Table Mountain National Park, South Africa
This national park was created in 1998 to protect the region's *fynbos* vegetation. The *fynbos* shrubland ecoregion, with its coastal Mediterranean climate, boasts about 6000 endemic plant species. The *fynbos*, which only covers a coastal strip 100–200km (60–120 miles) wide has extraordinary plant diversity, with over 9000 different species.

OPPOSITE:
Cape of Good Hope, Table Mountain National Park
Contrary to popular belief, the Cape of Good Hope is not the southernmost point of Africa: that is actually Cape Agulhas, around 150km (90 miles) to the southeast. For European sailors of the Age of Discovery, however, this was the hopeful point at which they began to sail more east than south.

PREVIOUS PAGE:
'Underwater waterfall',
Le Morne Brabant Peninsula, Mauritius
Visible only from above, the 'underwater waterfall' is actually an optical illusion. The island of Mauritius, in the Indian Ocean, sits on a large oceanic shelf, no deeper than 150m (490ft) below sea level. At the shelf's edge there is a drop-off point where the seabed suddenly plunges. However, it is not the water itself that we can see falling off this cliff: it is sand from Mauritius's beaches being forced over the ledge by ocean currents.

RIGHT:
Church of St George, Lalibela, Ethiopia
This cross-shaped Ethiopian Orthodox Tewahedo church was hewn as a single block of stone from the tuff bedrock in the late 12th or early 13th century. The church, along with 10 others nearby, was ordered by King Gebre Mesqel Lalibela of Ethiopia, who sought to create a religious landscape representing an earthly and heavenly Jerusalem, signified by two groups of churches, divided by a trench representing the River Jordan.

OPPOSITE:
Virunga National Park, Democratic Republic of the Congo
The Virunga Mountains are home to one of the world's two populations of the critically endangered mountain gorilla. It is believed that around 1000 individuals remain, threatened by poaching, habitat loss, disease and local instability caused by war and unrest. With its long, thick fur, the mountain gorilla inhabits the cold cloud forests at altitudes of 2200–4300m (7200–14,100ft).

Serengeti National Park, Tanzania

The Serengeti National Park encompasses vast grassland plains, as well as woodlands and forest. The region is famous for the annual migration in search of grazing of 1.5 million blue wildebeest (pictured above), as well as 470,000 Thomson's and Grant's gazelle, 250,000 plains zebra, and thousands of topi and Coke's hartebeest. The Serengeti is also home to around 3000 lions (pictured left).

OPPOSITE:

Kilimanjaro, Tanzania

This 5895-m (19,341-ft) dormant volcano is Africa's highest mountain. Despite its location close to the equator, the mountain's peak is covered by an ice cap, which has shrunk by 85 per cent since 1912. If global warming continues at the current rate, the ice will be gone by 2060. Kilimanjaro has three volcanic cones, the tallest being Kibo. The other two, Mawenzi and Shira, are extinct.

OPPOSITE:
Great Mosque of Djenné, Mali
Built in 1907 in traditional Sudano-Sahelian style, the walls of
this mosque are made of sun-baked mudbricks, sandwiched
with sand and mud mortar then plastered with mud. Sticks of
rodier palm, called *toron*, project from the structure, serving as
scaffolding for the necessary annual repairs. These repairs take
place during a festival involving the entire community.

ABOVE:
Djinguereber Mosque, Timbuktu, Mali
Largely made from mud, straw and wood, this 14th-century
mosque was constructed on the orders of Musa I (c. 1280–1337),
ruler of the Mali Empire. Musa, one of the richest people in the
history of the world due to his empire's gold mines, was also a
devout Muslim who made a pilgrimage to distant Mecca
in 1324–1325.

ABOVE:

Great Zimbabwe, Zimbabwe

Constructed from the 11th century, this walled city was once home to 18,000 Gokomere people, ancestors to the modern Shona. Following the end of white minority rule in 1980, Rhodesia was renamed Zimbabwe (from the Shona words for 'large stone houses') after the monument. One elliptical structure in the city, known as the Great Enclosure, has walls 11m (36ft) high with a circumference of 250m (820ft), forming the largest ancient structure south of the Sahara.

OPPOSITE:

Independence Arch, Accra, Ghana

Situated on Black Star Square, also known as Independence Square, in Ghana's capital city of Accra, this arch was commissioned to celebrate independence from the United Kingdom in 1957. The arch shows the influence of both Modernist and Soviet architecture. Black Star Square is the second largest square in the world, after Tiananmen Square in China's Beijing, and was designed to accommodate public events and military parades.

Victoria Falls, Zambia–Zimbabwe
This 108-m (355-ft) high waterfall on the Zambezi River is known as Mosi-oa-Tunya ('The Smoke that Thunders') in the local Lozi language. The Scottish explorer David Livingstone, probably the first European to view the falls, gave the feature its English name in honour of his queen. The falls are neither the highest nor the widest in the world, but they do form the largest sheet of falling water, due to the combined width 1708m (5604ft) and height.

Europe

Stretching from Iceland in the northwest to the Ural and Caucasus Mountains in the east, the continent of Europe hosts wild geographical extremes within a small, densely populated area. Rugged mountain ranges, such as the Alps, Pyrenees and Carpathians, quickly give way to fertile plains and river valleys. In the south, the Mediterranean Sea laps at the shores of countless jewel-like islands, while in the north, fjords have carved their way into the dramatic coasts of Scandinavia. Volcanic activity has marked the landscape and its people, from the Giant's Causeway of Northern Ireland to the buried cities of Pompeii and Herculaneum, forever in the shadow of Mount Vesuvius.

Around 3000 years ago, Europe was the birthplace of Western civilization and the ideals that went with it, from democracy to jurisprudence. We can still marvel at the monuments to order, ambition and ingenuity that the ancients left behind: from the temples of Athens' Acropolis to Roman aqueducts and amphitheatres. A few hundred years later, the stonemasons of northern Europe sent Gothic cathedrals soaring skyward. Then came the flowering of creativity that was the Renaissance, first taking root in Italy. Later, human imagination took myriad forms across the continent, from the sinuous shapes of Antoni Gaudí's Sagrada Família to the dream ship of Frank Gehry's Guggenheim Bilbao.

OPPOSITE:
St Basil's Cathedral, Moscow, Russia
Built on the orders of Ivan the Terrible in 1555–61, this one-time Russian Orthodox church on Moscow's Red Square has been used by the State Historical Museum since 1928. The seemingly chaotic cluster of multicoloured domes hides an organized interior: the tent-roofed central tower houses the main church, while the four largest domes, at the four compass points, top four octagonal towered chapels, with four additional cuboid chapels in between.

FAR LEFT:

Duomo, Florence, Italy
In 1418, the architect Filippo Brunelleschi won a competition to design the dome of Florence's cathedral. The extraordinary feat of engineering that he accomplished before his death in 1446 was the result of his intuition, complex maths and scale models. The octagonal dome was higher and wider than any previously built, and had to be constructed without external buttresses to prevent it spreading and collapsing.

LEFT:

West façade, Duomo
A competition to decorate the western façade of the cathedral was won in 1871 by Emilio de Fabris. The result was a neo-Gothic embellishment in red, green and white marble, in keeping with Giotto's richly decorated 14th-century Gothic belltower.

PREVIOUS PAGE:

Grand Canal, Venice, Italy

Venice's main waterway forms a large reverse S-shape through the city's central districts, from Cannaregio to San Marco. The canal is lined with more than 170 buildings, including many beautiful *palazzi* constructed by the city's wealthy and powerful from the 13th to the 18th centuries. Only four bridges cross the canal, including the famous Rialto Bridge and the most recent, the Ponte della Costituzione, designed in 2008 by Santiago Calatrava.

BELOW AND OPPOSITE:

Colosseum, Rome, Italy

This oval amphitheatre was the largest ever built, with room for 50,000 to 80,000 spectators. Construction began on the orders of the Emperor Vespasian in 82 AD, and was continued by his two sons, the emperors Titus and Domitian. The building was used for dramatic public spectacles, including gladiator fights, mock sea battles, animal hunts and executions. The *hypogeum* (below-ground areas) added by Domitian consisted of tunnels, cages and storerooms for gladiators, animals and scenery.

Pompeii, Campania, Italy

The eruption of Vesuvius in 79 AD buried the city of Pompeii under a layer of ash and pumice between 4 and 6m (13–20ft) thick. It was this layer, keeping out air and moisture, that preserved the city until its excavation, starting in 1748. Today, we can walk through the remains of the forum, temples, theatre, odeon, gymnasium, brothels, shops and homes.

Garden of the Fugitives, Pompeii

At the time of its destruction, 20,000 people lived in Pompeii. It is believed that around 2000 of them were unable to escape the city before being caught in the immense heat of a pyroclastic flow. The bodies of some of the victims left hollows in the hardened ash, which have been filled with plaster by archeologists. This may be the last resting place of a family.

FAR LEFT:

Leaning Tower of Pisa, Italy
The campanile (or free-standing belltower) of Pisa's 11th-century cathedral, the Leaning Tower was begun in 1173. It started to tilt almost immediately, due to poor foundations and soft, uneven ground. The increasing tilt was halted and stabilized through intensive engineering works in 1990–2001. Currently, the tower leans by around 4 degrees.

LEFT:

Leaning Tower of Pisa
The white marble tower has seven storeys, plus a bell chamber at the top, finally added in 1372 in a Gothic style that succeeds in harmonizing with the Romanesque style of the lower floors. The bottom storey has a blind arcade of 15 arches, while the next six floors have 30 arches each. The upper storeys are slightly curved, due to efforts by the architects to prevent the tower falling over. A 296-step spiral staircase leads to the top.

RIGHT:

Matterhorn, Switzerland–Italy

The 4478-m (14,692-ft) peak has four steep faces that face the four points of the compass. Little snow clings to these sheer faces, but instead falls in regular avalanches to the glaciers at the base. The mountain's forbidding shape is the result of erosion by several diverging glaciers.

FAR RIGHT:

Geirangerfjord, Møre og Romsdal, Norway

Geiranger is a 15-km (9-mile) branch of the vast Storfjorden (Great Fjord). Its steep cliffs are typical of the nearly 1200 fjords along Norway's coast. These U-shaped valleys were carved by glaciers then flooded by the sea.

Aurora, Lofoten, Norway
The aurora borealis, or
northern lights, can be seen
in the Lofoten archipelago of
Norway's Arctic Circle during
winter, from late August to
early April. The dancing lights
are caused by electrically
charged particles from the
Sun colliding with gaseous
particles in the Earth's
atmosphere. The charged
particles are mostly deflected
by the Earth's magnetic field,
except around the poles,
where the field is weaker.

Chartres Cathedral, France
Constructed largely
between 1194 and 1220, this
masterpiece of French Gothic
and Romanesque architecture
has two contrasting spires.
The plainer spire (seen here
at the front) was completed
in the 12th century, while the
other was added in the early
16th century in the late Gothic
style known as Flamboyant.
The south rose window (one
of three) has survived since
1225–30.

RIGHT:

Clock, Chartres Cathedral
The 24-hour clock, with a ray
of the sun for each half hour,
was added to the north façade
in 1520. It was built, with its
own pavilion, alongside the
Flamboyant spire, after the
original northern tower was
struck by lightning. The clock
is still in working order today.

LEFT:

Notre-Dame, Paris, France
Situated on Paris's Île de la Cité, this harmonious Gothic cathedral was begun in 1160 and largely completed over the next century. Its twin 13th-century towers and spire, which was rebuilt to the original design in the 19th century, soar over the surrounding city.

FAR LEFT:

Gargoyles, Notre-Dame
The cathedral's exterior statuary was intended as a 'book' for the people of Paris, who were largely illiterate. The many gargoyles, as well as chimeras (with the body of a lion and the head of a goat) and strixes (winged creatures that feed on human flesh), were warnings of the evil that waited for those who did not follow the teachings of the Church. The gargoyles also serve the practical purpose of being rainspouts, to project rain from the roof away from the structure and its mortar.

**Millau Viaduct,
Aveyron, France**
The tallest bridge in the
world, with a height of
343m (1125ft), this road
bridge was designed by
English architect Norman
Foster and French engineer
Michel Virlogeux. The bridge
deck is supported by steel
cables that stretch from
seven masts, each topping
a concrete pylon.

RIGHT:

Cologne Cathedral, Germany

With a height of 157m (515ft), this Catholic cathedral is the tallest twin-spired church in the world. Work began in the Gothic style in 1248. Although the south façade (pictured) was designed in the 13th century, work on it did not start until the 19th century. The flying buttresses (supports that slant outward from the main structure to a large pier) are a hallmark of Gothic architecture. They carry the outward thrust of the walls down to the ground.

FAR RIGHT:

West portal, Cologne Cathedral

Including its gable, this portal is more than 28m (92ft) high. The central, 19th-century statue on the trumeau (dividing pillar) is Mary. Above her, the arch-shaped tympanum shows scenes from the Old and New Testaments, from the Fall of Man at the top to scenes from the life of Christ at the bottom. The sculptures that fan out to either side were added in the 19th century.

RIGHT:

Sagrada Família, Barcelona, Spain

This unfinished Catholic church is one of the extraordinary works of Catalan architect Antoni Gaudí, who took over the project in 1883. When Gaudí was run over and killed by a streetcar in 1926, only one-quarter of the work was complete. It is hoped the building will be finished by 2026, to coincide with the anniversary of Gaudí's death. Gaudí was a leading architect of the Catalan Modernisme style, which synthesized Modernist ideas with neo-Gothic and Oriental influences – but in Gaudí's case was expressed through otherworldly, sinuous, twisting organic forms.

Trencadís, Parc Güell, Barcelona, Spain
Another of Gaudí's masterpieces in Barcelona
is the Parc Güell, a public park that was
originally intended as a housing development.
On the park's serpentine terrace bench, Gaudí
showcased the folk art technique of trencadís,
which uses tile and chinaware shards.

Parc Güell
The two gatehouses that flank the entrance to
the park are reminiscent of Hansel and Gretel-
style gingerbread houses. Their fantastical
roofs are topped with mushroom-shaped
domes and one (pictured here) boasts a spire
with a Greek cross.

Segovia Aqueduct, Spain
Probably constructed on the orders of the Emperor Domitian in around 98 AD, this is one of the best-preserved Roman aqueducts. It carried water to the city from the River Frio, with the decanted water running through a channel in its upper level. The granite blocks were unmortared.

ABOVE:
Guggenheim Museum Bilbao, Spain
This modern art museum, completed in 1997, was designed by Canadian-American architect Frank Gehry. The curving, seemingly random forms, clad in titanium, are designed to catch the light and to reflect the Nervión River.

OPPOSITE RIGHT:
Interior, Guggenheim Museum Bilbao
The curvilinear forms continue in the atrium and exhibition halls, creating intimate spaces to enjoy the art without feeling overwhelmed by the immensity of the construction. Glass walls and skylights flood the interior with light.

OPPOSITE FAR RIGHT:
Exterior, Guggenheim Museum Bilbao
The 73 spheres of Anish Kapoor's 2009 sculpture *Tall Tree and the Eye*, installed outside the museum, reflect the shining surfaces of the museum, the river, and the surrounding cityscape.

Erechtheion, Acropolis of Athens, Greece

This 5th-century BC temple to Athena and Poseidon is on the north side of Athens' Acropolis, a citadel on a rocky outcrop first inhabited up to 6000 years ago. On the temple's south side is a porch supported by six sculpted female figures, architectural features known as caryatids (literally 'maidens of Karyai', an ancient town on the Peloponnese). These sculptures are replicas: five of the originals are in the Acropolis Museum, while the sixth, removed by Lord Elgin, is in London's British Museum.

Parthenon, Acropolis of Athens

Built in the 5th century BC, this temple to the goddess Athena is considered the most perfect surviving example of the Doric order, the earliest and purest of the styles of classical Greek architecture. The temple has 17 columns down each side, with a double row of columns at either end, supporting a gable with a triangular pediment, on which were originally sculpted figures.

Stari Most, Mostar, Bosnia and Herzegovina
Originally completed in 1567 when the region was ruled by the Ottoman Empire, this elegant arched bridge over the River Neretva is a masterpiece of Balkan Islamic architecture. The bridge was destroyed in 1993 during the Bosnian War, but rebuilt to the original design using Ottoman construction techniques.

OPPOSITE:

Meteora, Thessaly, Greece
Meteora (from the Greek for 'lofty') is the name for a group of eroded sandstone columns that rise precipitously from the Plain of Thessaly. During the 11th to 16th centuries, a total of 24 monasteries were built on the columns, of which six remain. Access to the monasteries was deliberately difficult: monks, pilgrims and supplies had to be hoisted up in nets in a process that truly demanded deep faith in God.

LEFT:

Plitvice Lakes National Park, Croatia
Situated in the mountainous limestone and dolomite karst landscape of central Croatia, this park protects 16 interconnected lakes, separated by natural dams made of travertine. Brown bears, wolves, lynxes and wild cats can be found in the surrounding forest.

RIGHT:

Dubrovnik, Croatia
This port city reached the pinnacle of its wealth in the 15th and 16th centuries. The city walls and many fine Renaissance churches, palaces, squares, stairways and fountains have more recently stood in for King's Landing in the fantasy television series *Game of Thrones*.

Pena Palace, Sintra, Portugal
Built for King Ferdinand II
between 1842 and 1854, this
dramatic castle was concocted
in the Romanticist style,
evoking an idealized medieval
past. The buildings, complete
with drawbridge, feature a
profusion of influences,
from Moorish arches to
Gothic windows.

OPPOSITE:

Pena Palace
The palace stands on a
rocky hilltop in the Sintra
Mountains, on the site of a
monastery ruined by the Great
Lisbon Earthquake of 1755.
The bright colours of the
façade have been repainted to
match the original scheme.

OPPOSITE:

Jökulsárlón, southeastern Iceland

Currently covering 18 sq km (6.9 sq miles), this lake was created by the melting of Breiðamerkurjökull, a tongue of the vast ice cap Vatnajökull. The lake first developed in around 1948 and has grown fourfold since 1970. If Breiðamerkurjökull continues to retreat, the lake will eventually become a fjord.

ABOVE:

Jökulsárlón and Breiðamerkurjökull

Breiðamerkurjökull is one of around 30 outlet glaciers of Vatnajökull, which is the largest glacier in Europe by volume, covering 8 per cent of Iceland's surface. There are several volcanoes under the ice cap, which regularly erupt, resulting in sudden flooding.

Øresund Bridge, Denmark–Sweden

This combined rail and road bridge stretches 7845m (25,738ft) across the Øresund Strait between Sweden and Denmark. The rail tracks are on a girder beneath the road deck. The majority of the structure is supported by concrete piers, but a central cable-stayed section allows greater head room for shipping to pass through. The western end of the bridge comes to a stop at the artificial island of Peberholm, from where a 4-km (2.5-mile) tunnel completes the journey.

Giant's Causeway, County Antrim, Northern Ireland
The Giant's Causeway is made up of 40,000 basalt columns, formed 50 to 60 million years ago as a massive eruption of lava cooled and cracked, the network of cracks forming a regular pattern. Most of the columns are hexagonal, but some have four, five, seven or eight sides.

LEFT:
Giant's Causeway
Legend has it that the volcanic feature was built by the Irish giant Fionn mac Cumhaill. After being challenged to a fight by the Scottish giant Benandonner, Fionn constructed the causeway over the sea to reach him. In reality, the same immense lava flow that created the Giant's Causeway also formed the basalt columns at Fingal's Cave on the Scottish island of Staffa, a fact that may well have influenced the story.

LEFT:

Cliffs of Moher, County Clare, Ireland

These dramatic cliffs of sandstone and shale extend for 14km (9 miles) along Ireland's Atlantic coast. They reach 214m (702ft) at their highest point, near O'Brien's Tower (pictured here). The tower was built by local MP Sir Cornelius O'Brien in 1835 as an observation point and teahouse for tourists. During the breeding season, the cliffs are home to 30,000 pairs of birds, including Atlantic puffins.

ABOVE:

Hadrian's Wall, Northern England

This wall, built to protect the province of Britannia from 'barbarians' such as the Picts to the north, was begun on the orders of Roman Emperor Hadrian in 122 AD. Along its 118-km (73-mile) length, there was a fort every 5000 paces, or five Roman miles. For every mile in between, there was a smaller fortlet, such as the one pictured here, with room for a few dozen troops.

FOLLOWING PAGE:

Stonehenge, Wiltshire, England

The ring of standing stones and earthworks known as Stonehenge was built between 3000 and 2000 BC, with the surrounding bank and ditch part of the earliest phase of construction. The inner horseshoe of stones is designed to coincide with sunrise at the midsummer solstice. This has led some to believe that Stonehenge is a giant calendar, while others think the site was used for sacrifices or other rituals.

The Americas

The Americas are breathtaking in the scale of their landscapes. Here we find the world's longest above-sea mountain range, the Andes; the biggest river, the Amazon, snaking its way across South America; and the largest rainforest, home to one in ten known species. The powerful forces that shape our planet can be appreciated in the dramatically eroded landscapes of the USA's Monument Valley and Arches National Park, as well as the volcanic plugs of the Caribbean's Pitons and the steaming springs of Yellowstone. Testament to the fragility of our beautiful planet are the retreating glaciers of Canada's Glacier National Park and Chile's Torres del Paine.

For millennia, the Americas were home to complex civilizations that bequeathed us many extraordinary monuments. In North America, we can visit the cliff dwellings of the ancestral Puebloans; in Central America, the step pyramids of the Maya and Teotihuacans; in South America, the temples of the Tiwanaku Empire, the citadels of the Inca and the mysterious geoglyphs of the Nazca culture. Indigenous peoples were decimated by the arrival of Europeans, who set about putting their stamp on the continent, from the colonial-era ports of Valparaíso, Havana and Willemstad, to the engineering achievements of modern times, from the Golden Gate Bridge to the Empire State Building.

OPPOSITE:
Grand Canyon from Toroweap Overlook, Arizona, USA
The remote Toroweap Overlook, on the North Rim, is the only viewpoint on the canyon where the Colorado River can be seen directly below. The canyon was carved out by the river over the last 5 to 6 million years. Layers of different sedimentary rocks, including shale, sandstone and limestone, can be seen in the canyon walls, with the oldest dating back 1.8 billion years.

Hoover Dam, Arizona–Nevada, USA

Completed in 1936, this concrete dam in the Black Canyon of the Colorado River formed Lake Mead. With a volume of 32.22 cu km (7.7 cu miles) when full, Mead is the largest reservoir by volume in the USA, although it has not been full since 1983. The dam's power station generates, on average, 4.2 terawatt hours per year, enough electricity for about 350,000 homes. Sadly, more than 100 workers died during the construction of the dam.

Delicate Arch, Arches National Park, Utah, USA
This 18-m (60-ft) freestanding sandstone arch was formed by weathering and erosion, along with another 2000 arches in the park. The process of arch formation begins when water seeps into an exposed fin of rock. When the water freezes, the expanding ice cracks the rock, then loose grains are carried away by wind and rain. The snow-capped La Sal Mountains can be seen in the distance.

Devil's Tower, Wyoming, USA
Geologists are not all in agreement, but it is likely that this National Monument formed around 40 million years ago when magma cooled inside the vent of a volcano, creating a plug of phonolite. The softer rock surrounding the phonolite was eroded away. The butte is the subject of many Native American myths, with the English name for the site a mistranslation dating back to 1875.

ABOVE:

Cliff Palace, Mesa Verde National Park, Colorado, USA
The largest cliff dwelling in North America was built by the ancestral Puebloans from sandstone,
wood and mud mortar between 1190 and 1260 AD. Chosen for its defensive position, the site was
later abandoned because of drought. The complex was home to around 100 people in numerous
dwelling rooms. There were also 23 *kivas*, round sunken rooms with a ceremonial purpose.

OPPOSITE:

Grand Prismatic Spring, Yellowstone National Park, Wyoming, USA
Heated by the underlying Yellowstone Caldera, the continent's largest supervolcano, this is the
biggest hot spring in the USA. Half the world's geysers and other geothermal features are located
in Yellowstone, including the Steamboat and Old Faithful geysers. The bright colours around the
edges of the spring are created by microbial mats that grow in the warm, mineral-rich water.

PREVIOUS PAGE:

**Mount Rushmore,
South Dakota, USA**

Local historian Doane Robinson had the idea of creating a monumental carving in the Black Hills, featuring Buffalo Bill, to attract tourism. Sculptor Gutzon Borglum decided the sculpture should instead depict four presidents (left to right): George Washington, Thomas Jefferson, Theodore Roosevelt and Abraham Lincoln. Work began in 1927, continuing until funds ran out in 1941. The original plan had been to depict the presidents from head to waist.

RIGHT:

**Yosemite National Park,
California, USA**

The glaciers that carved Yosemite Valley also left many hanging valleys, high valleys carved by tributary glaciers. These are the sources for many of Yosemite's waterfalls, including Bridalveil Fall, on the other side of the main valley from the granite monolith El Capitan.

OPPOSITE:

**Monument Valley,
Arizona–Utah, USA**

The tallest of Monument Valley's much filmed and photographed buttes reaches 300m (1000ft) from the floor of the Colorado Plateau. The buttes, sometimes exhibiting a finger or 'mitten' shape, are the eroded remains of a vast sandstone deposit.

Golden Gate Bridge, San Francisco, California, USA
Constructed in 1933–37, this suspension bridge is a road and foot link across the Golden Gate, the strait separating San Francisco Bay from the Pacific Ocean. The graceful Art Deco bridge, designed and engineered by Irving Morrow, Joseph Strauss and Charles Ellis, is painted a shade called International Orange, also used by NASA, because it is easily seen in fog but complements the landscape.

Zabriskie Point, Death Valley National Park, California, USA

This eroded landscape is composed of sedimentary rocks, the cemented deposits of mud, gravel and ash from the bottom of Furnace Creek Lake, which covered this area between 9 and 5 million years ago. After the climate became more arid and the lake dried up, gullies and rills were eroded into the soft rock by the streams that rushed down the slopes after heavy rain.

Empire State Building, New York, USA

This 102-storey, 381-m (1250-ft) skyscraper was the world's tallest building from its completion in 1931 until the North Tower of the World Trade Center was completed in 1970. On 11 September 2001, it again became New York's tallest building, until One World Trade Center (also pictured at far right) was completed in 2012. Developed by Empire State Inc. and designed in finely crafted Art Deco style by Shreve, Lamb & Harmon, the Empire State Building took only 13 months to erect. The sumptuously decorated lobby boasts an aluminium relief of the tower (pictured).

Statue of Liberty, New York, USA

Dedicated in 1886, this statue of Libertas, the Roman goddess of liberty, was a gift from France to the USA. The copper statue, 46m (151ft) tall, was designed by French sculptor Frédéric Auguste Bartholdi and built in Paris by engineer Gustave Eiffel, before being shipped to the USA and erected on a 47-m (154-ft) high pedestal. The cost of the pedestal was partly met by New Yorkers, who responded to a funding drive in the *New York World* newspaper, many of them giving the few cents they could afford. Across New York Harbor is another icon of the USA, One World Trade Center, its height of 1776ft (541.3m) a reference to the year when the Declaration of Independence was signed.

Niagara Falls, Ontario, Canada–New York, USA
These three waterfalls on the Niagara River lie on the US–Canada border. The largest of the three, Horseshoe Falls (pictured), with a height of 51m (167ft) and an awe-inspiring width of 820m (2700ft), takes 90 per cent of the river's flow. The remaining 10 per cent is shared by American Falls and the much smaller Bridal Veil Falls, which are both over the US border.

**Moraine Lake,
Banff National Park,
Alberta, Canada**
This glacially fed lake,
1885m (6183ft) above sea level,
is fullest in June. At this time
of year, the lake is its most
dazzling turquoise, a shade
created by the refraction of
light by the large quantities
of rock flour suspended in the
water. Rock flour is tiny grains
of rock, ground away from the
bedrock by glacial erosion.

**Illecillewaet River, Glacier
National Park, British
Columbia, Canada**
Meltwater from the
Illecillewaet Glacier forms
the Illecillewaet River. This
is just one of the 131 glaciers
in Glacier National Park, all
of them currently retreating.
Glaciers ancient and modern
have carved the park's many
steep-sided U-shaped valleys.
The park covers a range of
habitats, from alpine tundra,
through fir and pine forests,
to temperate rainforest in the
western valleys.

LEFT:

Caño Cristales, Colombia

Caño Cristales in Colombia's Serranía de la Macarena province is also known as the River of Five Colours, thanks to the brightly coloured aquatic plants that cling to cracks in the rocky riverbed. Largely free from sediment, the river water is unusually clear. The colours – including yellow, green, blue and, most often, red – are at their brightest after the rainy season, from July to November. The red is the result of endemic *Macarenia clavigera* riverweeds.

RIGHT:

Caño Cristales

The quartzite riverbed has been eroded into many waterfalls and circular pits, known as giants' kettles, by the flast-flowing water. Giants' kettles are created by the bumping of large rocks. Once a dent is created, the water current rotates rocks around the cavity, slowly enlarging it.

Temple I, Tikal

The burial place of *ajaw* (ruler) Jasaw Chan K'awiil in 734 AD, this funerary pyramid temple is 47m (154ft) high. The shrine at the summit of the pyramid is topped by a roofcomb that once sported a sculpture of Jasaw Chan K'awiil on his throne.

OPPOSITE:

North Acropolis, Tikal, Guatemala

The capital of one of the most powerful Maya kingdoms, Tikal was at the peak of its influence from 200 to 900 AD. During this time, the city may have had as many as 90,000 inhabitants. Today, we can admire the remains of limestone temples, palaces, ball courts, administrative buildings and homes. The North Acropolis, next to the Great Plaza, was a royal funeral complex, with successive rulers adding temple pyramids on top of previous structures.

Plaza of the Moon, Teotihuacan, Mexico

At its peak, around 450 AD, Teotihuacan was the largest city in the pre-Columbian Americas, with a population of 125,000. Teotihuacan's inhabitants may have been from several ethnic groups, including Totonac, Zapotec, Maya and Nahua. Today, the city is known for its giant stepped pyramids, as well as its many multi-storey apartment buildings. The Plaza of the Moon, in front of the Pyramid of the Moon, has 12 temple platforms.

Pyramid of the Moon, Teotihuacan

Built between 200 and 250 AD, the Pyramid of the Moon is the second largest pyramid in Teotihuacan, after the Pyramid of the Sun, which was probably complete when the Teotihuacans erected this sister pyramid. The Pyramid of the Moon is 43m (141ft) tall, while the other is 66m (217ft). A platform on top of the Pyramid of the Moon may have been used for ceremonies in honour of the Great Goddess of Teotihuacan.

RIGHT:

Panama Canal, Panama
One of the largest engineering works ever undertaken, the building of the Panama Canal lasted from 1881 to 1894 (by France) and 1904 to 1914 (by the USA) and may have cost as many as 27,000 lives as a result of disease and accidents. The canal was built to dramatically reduce the time taken to sail between the Atlantic and Pacific Oceans by cutting through the Isthmus of Panama. The canal is 26m (85ft) above sea level, to reduce excavation time, with locks at either end used to raise and lower vessels.

FAR RIGHT:

Amazon River, near Manaus, Brazil
The Amazon is the world's biggest river by discharge of water: 209,000 cu m/s (7,400,000 cu ft/s), which is larger than the discharge of the next seven largest rivers combined. Most geographers agree that the Amazon's source is the headwaters of the Mantaro River in Peru. Other tributaries are in Colombia and Ecuador. The great river winds for 6992.6 km (4345 miles) before meeting the Atlantic Ocean near Belém in Brazil.

Christ the Redeemer, Rio de Janeiro, Brazil
Carved from the soft metamorphic rock soapstone, the 38-m (125-ft) tall statue of *Christ the Redeemer* has a reinforced concrete core. It stands on Corcovado (from the Portuguese for 'hunchback'), a giant exposed block of granite known as a *bornhardt* and nicknamed a 'sugar loaf' for its shape. The Art Deco statue has watched over Rio de Janeiro since 1931, when it was created by a team including sculptors Paul Landowski and Gheorghe Leonida and engineers Heitor da Silva Costa and Albert Caquot.

LEFT:
Scarlet macaws, Amazon Rainforest, Brazil

Although still widespread in the Amazon, this large macaw is in decline due to habitat loss and the illegal pet trade. Scarlet macaws often gather at clay licks, from which they gather nutritionally important sodium. It is also believed that the toxins from seeds and unripe fruits eaten by the birds bind to the clay minerals in the macaws' stomachs, making them harmless.

RIGHT:
Iguazu Falls, Brazil–Argentina

With between 150 and 300 falls, depending on the water flow, and a total height of up to 82m (269ft), the Iguazu Falls are the world's largest waterfall system. The separate waterfalls are created by numerous islands along the 2.7-km (1.7-mile) edge.

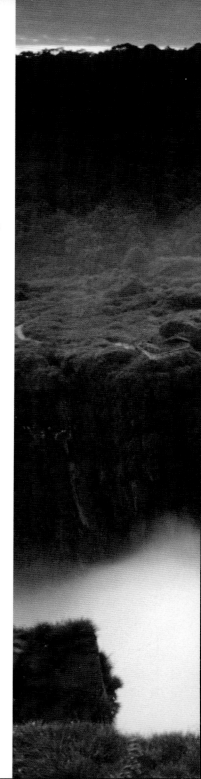

LEFT TOP AND BOTTOM:

Cueva de las Manos, Argentina

This series of caves is famous for its artwork, which was created by successive waves of inhabitants between 13,000 and 9500 years ago. Most of the many hands depicted are left hands, which suggests that the artists used their right hand to hold a pipe, through which they blew, spraying paint onto the wall around their outstretched left hand. The mineral pigments used include iron oxides (for red), kaolin (for white) and manganese oxide (for black).

RIGHT:

Los Cuernos, Torres del Paine National Park, Chile

Los Cuernos ('The Horns') are jagged peaks of shale, crowning paler granite. All higher than 2000m (6560ft), Los Cuernos are in Torres del Paine National Park, which lies in an eastern spur of the Andes Mountains and encompasses glaciers, rivers, lakes and habitats from Magellanic subpolar forest and Patagonian steppe to Andean desert.

OPPOSITE:

Marble Caves, Chile
Located on a peninsula of marble, the caves have been eroded by the waters of General Carrera Lake, Chile's largest lake, formed by glaciers amid the Andes Mountains. The cavern walls reflect the blue of the lake water, changing their tint and intensity depending on the season and time of day.

LEFT:

Valparaíso, Chile
Nicknamed the 'Jewel of the Pacific', this port city is built on steep hillsides, some of them climbed by funicular lifts. In the late 19th and early 20th centuries, the city was the key port on the Pacific Coast of South America on the route linking the Atlantic and Pacific Oceans via the Strait of Magellan. The brightly painted colonial houses, alleyways, promenades and squares were uniquely adapted to their amphitheatre-like setting.

Temple of Kalasasaya, Tiwanaku, Bolivia

The giant archeological site of Tiwanaku, near Lake Titicaca, probably dates back to 110 AD. At its peak, in around 800 AD, this city was home to 10,000–20,000 people. It was the political and spiritual centre of the Tiwanaku Empire, which covered northern Bolivia, southern Peru and western Chile. The excavated ruins cover only the ceremonial centres of the city: pyramids, temples and palaces built from giant stone blocks. The Temple of Kalasasaya is a low platform mound with a large, sunken central courtyard. The tenon heads jutting from the walls may represent the idols of peoples subject to the Tiwanaku.

OPPOSITE:
Salar de Uyuni, Bolivia

Covering 10,582 sq km (4086 sq miles), the Salar de Uyuni is the world's largest salt flat. High in the Altiplano, a plain surrounded by mountains with no drainage outlets, the salt flat formed by the evaporation of several ancient salt lakes. Beneath the crust is a layer of brine that is rich in lithium, a vital component of many batteries. In fact, it contains 50 to 70 per cent of the world's lithium reserves. The Bolivian government does not want the region exploited, so there is currently only very modest mining.

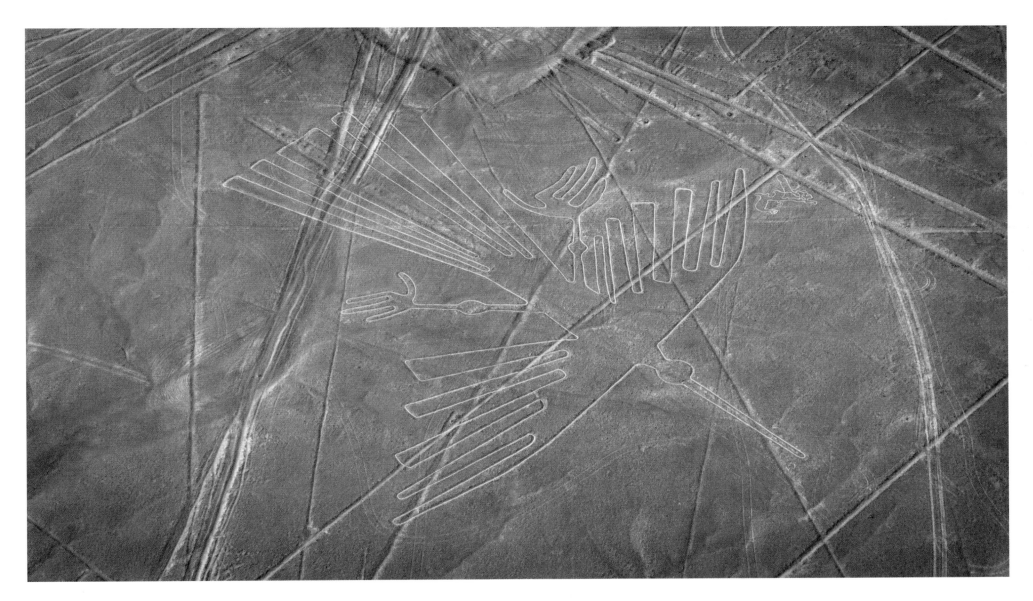

Angel Falls, Venezuela

With a straight drop of 807m (2648ft), Angel Falls is the world's highest uninterrupted waterfall. A second drop, rapids and a sloped cascade brings the falls' total height to 979m (3211ft). The waterfall plummets from Auyán Tepui, a tabletop mountain in the Guiana Highlands. Tepuis are isolated ecological islands known for their endemic plant and animal species, like mainland Galápagos Islands: Auyán Tepui hosts 25 endemic species of amphibians and reptiles alone.

Nazca Lines, Peru

The Nazca Lines are a series of geoglyphs in the desert of southern Peru, created between 500 BC and 500 AD. The designs are visible from the surrounding foothills, but are seen to most dramatic effect from the air. They were created by scraping away the top layer of reddish pebbles, revealing the paler subsoil. The geoglyphs, up to 1100m (3600ft) long, include trees, flowers and more than 70 animals, such as a hummingbird (pictured), monkey, dog, llama, fish, pelican and spider.

Machu Picchu, Peru
The Incas built the citadel of Machu Picchu in around 1450 but abandoned it a century later during the Spanish Conquest. It is possible that many of its inhabitants died from smallpox. Dramatically located on a ridge at a height of 2430m (7970ft), the citadel was probably built as an estate for the Inca ruler Pachacutec Inca Yupanqui, with no more than 750 family members, staff, workers and priests in residence at any one time. There were residences for different classes, warehouses, guardhouses and temples, all built from carefully hewn blocks of unmortared granite. Farming was carried out on terraces on the surrounding slopes (pictured on this page).

PREVIOUS PAGE:

Havana, Cuba

Founded by the Spanish in 1519, and a stopping-off point for their treasure-laden galleons, Old Havana was built in the Baroque and Neoclassical styles. The domed El Capitolio, constructed in the 1920s, was home to the Cuban Congress until the revolution of 1959. The Castillo de la Real Fuerza, near the waterfront at the far right, was completed in 1577 and is considered the oldest stone fort in the Americas.

BELOW:

Willemstad, Curaçao

The capital of Curaçao, a constituent country of the Netherlands, Willemstad was founded by the Dutch in 1634, after capturing the island from Spain. On the harbourfront, the yellow Penha Building (far right), constructed in 1708, clearly shows the influence of Dutch architecture. In the streets just behind is the 1730 Mikvé Israel-Emanuel Synagogue, the oldest surviving synagogue in the Americas.

OPPOSITE:

Pitons, St Lucia

These volcanic plugs on the southwestern coast of St Lucia are separated by Pitons Bay. Gros Piton (right) is 771m (2530ft), while Petit Piton (left) is 743m (2438ft). The volcanic complex that formed them also feeds fumaroles and hot springs. Both mountains are popular with walkers and climbers, but ropes are needed for Petit Piton. Gros Piton is home to 148 plant species and 27 bird species, five of them endemic.

Asia

Many of the wonders of Asia were built by devotees of the continent's three largest religions: Islam, Hinduism and Buddhism. We can still marvel at the skills and belief of the craftspeople who erected the mosques of Central Asia; the sacred landscape of the Hindu temple of Angkor Wat, which was later converted to Buddhism; and the world's largest Buddhist temple, at Borobudur, in Java. The spread of these religions carried not only ideas but architectural forms across the continent, including the dome-shaped stupas of India, designed to hold relics of the Buddha, which developed into multiple-eaved pagodas in their journey through Southeast and East Asia.

Some of the wonders of this continent were created not so much from faith as from a desire to leave a mark on the physical world. Among these extraordinary monuments to human ambition are the breathtakingly grandiose mausoleums of rulers such as Qin Shi Huang of China, Antiochus I Theos of Turkey, Timur of Central Asia and, perhaps most famous of all, Shah Jahan's tomb for his beloved wife, in India. Other Asian attempts to build longer, higher or more innovatively than ever before range from the Great Wall of China to the Supertrees of Singapore. Asia's wonders of the natural world are also record-breaking, from the planet's 100 tallest mountains to the hottest desert, the Dasht-e Lut.

OPPOSITE:

Ha Long Bay, Vietnam

According to legend, Ha Long, which means 'descending dragon' in Vietnamese, was created by a family of dragons sent to protect the nation from invaders. The dragons spat out jewels, which turned into rocks and islands, wrecking the invaders' ships. The geological explanation for the islands' formation is that they are the eroded remains of a limestone deposit.

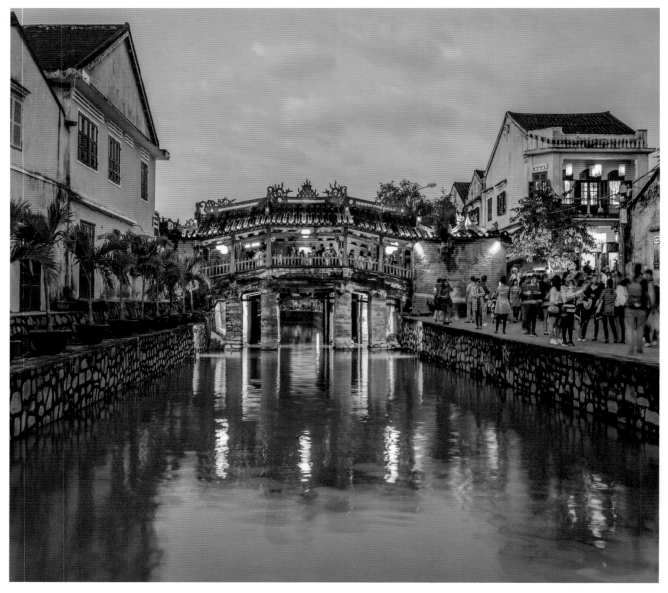

ABOVE:

Japanese Bridge, Hoi An, Vietnam
From the 16th to the 18th centuries, Hoi An was a key trading port for ships between Europe,
China, India and Japan, especially those carrying ceramics. Japanese merchants lived in their own
area of the city, over the covered 'Japanese Bridge'. At either end, the bridge is guarded by statues
of monkeys and dogs, which are probably references to animals of the Chinese zodiac.

ABOVE:

Old Quarter, Hoi An
Hoi An's riverside Old Quarter shows the influences of the
Chinese, Japanese, Vietnamese and European traders who once
made their living here. In its narrow lanes are 200-year-old
merchants' houses, tea warehouses and Chinese assembly halls.

LEFT:

Gate of Angkor Thom, Cambodia

The last and longest-lasting capital of the Khmer Empire, Angkor Thom was built a little to the southeast, and overlapping with, the previous capital of Yasodharapura. The city walls enclose an area of 9 sq km (3.5 sq miles). The north, south, east and west gates are sculpted with faces that may represent King Jayavarman VII, founder of the city, or a *bodhisattva* (a godlike being).

FAR LEFT:

Angkor Wat, Cambodia

One of the largest religious complexes in the world, Angkor Wat was built as a Hindu temple in the early 12th century by Suryavarman II, in the capital of the Khmer Empire, Yasodharapura. Later that century, the wat became a Buddhist temple. The complex was designed as a 'temple mountain' representing Mount Meru, home of the gods. The towers symbolize the five peaks of Meru, while the walls and moat represent the encircling mountain ranges and ocean.

Petronas Towers, Kuala Lumpur, Malaysia

From their completion in 1998 until 2004, when they were overtaken by Taipei 101 in Taiwan, the Petronas Towers were the world's tallest buildings. The 451.9-m (1483-ft) twin towers were designed by Argentine architect César Pelli, with the towers' cross-section resembling a Rub el Hizb, an Islamic symbol of two overlapping squares. The skybridge, connecting the 41st and 42nd floors of the two buildings, is not attached to the main structure, so it is free to slide back and forwards a little as the towers sway in high winds.

Supertree Grove, Gardens by the Bay, Singapore
The Gardens by the Bay were opened in 2008, as part of Singapore's plan to improve quality of life in the city state by creating new green spaces and improving air quality. The 25- to 50-m (82–160-ft) Supertrees are vertical gardens that do exactly that. As well as being home to vines, orchids and bromeliads, they collect rainwater for irrigation and fountains; hold solar cells to power lighting; and house cooling systems for the gardens' greenhouses.

ABOVE:
Borobudur, Java, Indonesia
The largest Buddhist temple in the world, Borobudur was built in the 9th century. It consists of six stacked square platforms, topped by three circular ones. Pilgrims to the temple ascend a path through three realms: Kamadhatu (the world of desire), Rupadhatu (the world of forms) and Arupadhatu (the world of formlessness), the story told through 1460 relief panels.

RIGHT:
Upper platform, Borobudur
The ninth platform is home to 72 small stupas (hemispherical structures usually containing relics), surrounding a large central stupa. Each small stupa is bell-shaped and pierced by a latticework of carving, with a statue of the Buddha at its centre. Together they represent Arupadhatu. The main stupa is empty, symbolizing the complete perfection of enlightenment.

Bagan, Myanmar

From the 9th to the 13th centuries, Bagan was the capital of the Pagan Kingdom, which covered the region of modern Myanmar. More than 10,000 Buddhist temples, monasteries and pagodas (tiered towers that developed from the form of the South Asian stupa) were constructed in and around the city, of which over 2000 remain.One of the most famous is the Ananda Temple (pictured close to the centre of the near right photo), built in 1105 in a cruciform shape. The temple is topped by a small pagoda crowned by a *hti*, an umbrella-like finial.

PREVIOUS PAGE:
Great Wall of China
The majority of the existing Great Wall dates back to the Ming Dynasty (1368–1644), although parts were built by the first emperor, Qin Shi Huang (247–220 BC), and the structure has its origins in walls built in the 7th century BC. The guiding principle of the Great Wall, which consists of stretches of stone fortification, trenches, tamped earth and natural barriers, was to keep out invaders from the Eurasian steppe. The entire wall, in all its forms and branches, stretches an incredible 21,196km (13,171 miles) according to some surveys.

LEFT AND FAR LEFT:
Longmen Caves, Henan, China
These 2345 man-made caves, along the east and west sides of the Yi River, contain 100,000 statues of the Buddha and his disciples, carved as reliefs on the limestone cliffs outside and hewn from the internal walls. The caves were excavated and decorated between 493 and 1127 AD. Fengxian Cave (pictured) is the largest open-air niche, carved between 672 and 676 for Empress Wu Zetian. The cross-legged Buddha is 17.14m (56ft) high, with ears 2m (6.6ft) long.

RIGHT:

Infantrymen, Terracotta Army, Shaanxi, China

These life-size terracotta statues were placed in a series of pits near the mausoleum of the first emperor of a unified China, Qin Shi Huang, in 210–209 BC. The 8000 soldiers, 130 chariots, 670 horses, plus officials, acrobats and musicians were intended to protect and serve the emperor in the afterlife. The Terracotta Army, rediscovered in 1974, is actually only one part of a vast underground necropolis, covering 98 sq km (38 sq miles), designed as a replica of the emperor's palace and compound.

FAR RIGHT:

Kneeling archer, Terracotta Army

Many different types and ranks of warriors are portrayed, from kneeling, armoured archers to pillbox-hat-wearing cavalrymen, helmeted chariot drivers, officers and generals. The sculptors went to great efforts to individualize each soldier, with different clothing and each face apparently unique, although they appear to be based on ten standard face shapes. The original bright paint, which would have lent further individuality, has mostly flaked off.

**Forbidden City,
Beijing, China**
Home to China's emperors
from 1420 to 1912, this palace
contains 980 buildings. The
English name, translated from
the Chinese *Jen* ('forbidden'),
refers to the fact that no
one could enter without
the emperor's permission.
The complex is surrounded
by a moat and a wall with
corner towers with elaborate
multiple-ridged roofs.

Himeji Castle, Honshu, Japan
The finest and largest surviving example of a Japanese feudal castle, Himeji is often called Shirasagi-jo ('White Heron Castle') because of its resemblance to a white bird in flight. The first castle on the site was erected in 1333, but was much remodelled and extended over the years. The current incarnation dates from 1618. The central gabled keep, made of wood and stone, has six storeys. To reach it, the visitor must navigate a maze of walled paths, gates and baileys, designed to slow and expose attackers. Inside the keep (pictured opposite), each storey is progressively smaller. There are weapons racks, hiding spaces for warriors and stone-throwing platforms.

167

Mount Fuji, Honshu, Japan
Reflected here in Lake
Kawaguchiko, Mount Fuji
is Japan's highest mountain,
reaching 3776m (12,389ft).
Just 100km (60 miles) from
the megacity of Tokyo, Fuji
is an active stratovolcano that
last erupted in 1707–08. The
volcano is snow-capped in
winter, but the lower slopes
are cloaked with Japanese and
konara beech, Nikko fir and
mizunara oak.

LEFT:

Kinkaku-ji, Kyoto, Honshu, Japan

Kinkaku-ji, which translates as 'Temple of the Golden Pavilion', is a Zen Buddhist temple first built in 1397 and reconstructed in 1955 after a fire. The top two storeys are covered in gold leaf. Each storey of the pavilion showcases a different architectural style. The ground floor, in shinden style, is evocative of 10th- and 11th-century imperial palaces, with unpainted wood to emphasize the natural surroundings. The middle floor is in the style of residences for military, or samurai, families. The top floor is in the style of a Zen temple. The Zen school of Buddhism emphasizes meditation rather than ritual worship or scriptures.

RIGHT:

Todai-ji, Nara, Honshu, Japan

The current temple was rebuilt after a fire in 1709. The first temple on the site was erected in the 8th century, when Nara was the imperial capital. The Great Buddha Hall (pictured) houses the world's largest bronze statue of the Buddha Vairocana (the universal Buddha, a personification of the illumination of wisdom), which is 14.98m (49ft 2in) tall.

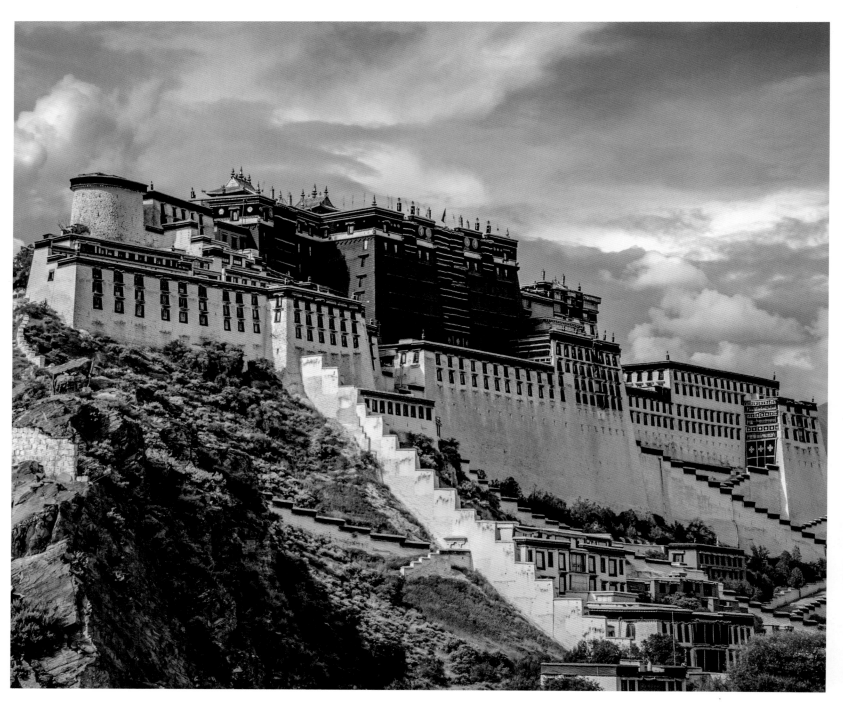

Potala Palace, Lhasa, Tibet
The Potala Palace was home
to the Dalai Lama until the
current Dalai Lama, the 14th,
fled to India during the 1959
Tibetan Uprising. The Dalai
Lama is the spiritual leader
of the Tibetan people and of
the Gelug school of Tibetan
Buddhism. Work on the palace
was begun in 1645 by the fifth
Dalai Lama. Poised on the
Marpo Ri ('Red Hill'), the
complex has 13 storeys, more
than 1000 rooms and around
10,000 shrines.

OPPOSITE:

**Patan Durbar Square,
Lalitpur, Nepal**
This is one of three durbar
squares in the Kathmandu
Valley. These squares, situated
outside the entrances to
the palaces of the old royal
kingdoms, contain temples,
shrines and fountains. The
temples of Patan Durbar
Square date from the 17th
century, all built in the style of
traditional Newa architecture
and featuring intricate wood
carving and brickwork.

Mount Everest and Nuptse, Himalayas, China–Nepal

Photographed from the slopes of Kala Patthar, Mount Everest (left) looks lower than Nuptse (to the right). Nuptse is in fact only 7861m (25,791ft), while Everest is the world's highest mountain at 8848m (29,029ft). The first climbers to reach the summit of Everest were the Nepali-Indian Sherpa Tenzing Norgay and New Zealander Edmund Hillary, in 1953.

ABOVE:

Shalimar Gardens, Lahore, Pakistan

These Mughal gardens were created in 1641–2, during the reign of Shah Jahan. They were laid out according to the principles of the Persian paradise garden, using a rectlinear, formal plan and extensive water features to represent the four gardens of Paradise.

OPPOSITE:

Mohenjo-Daro, Sindh, Pakistan

Mohenjo-Daro was one of the great cities of the Indus Valley civilization, which thrived from around 3200 to 1700 BC. Mohenjo-Daro had monumental public buildings, including the 'Great Bath' containing a large pool, an extensive sewer system and homes with bathrooms and toilets.

LEFT:
**Chor Minor,
Bukhara, Uzbekistan**
A great city of the Silk Road,
Bukhara was also a major
intellectual centre of the
Islamic world during the
9th and 10th centuries. The
Chor Minor mosque is one of
the more recent of the city's
many mosques and madrasas
(religious schools), dating
from 1807.

OPPOSITE:
**Gate of Gur-e-Amir,
Samarkand, Uzbekistan**
Gur-e-Amir (Persian for
'Tomb of the King') is the
mausoleum of Timur (1336–
1405), a Turco-Mongol
conqueror whose descendants
founded the Mughal dynasty
and ruled over much of
the Indian subcontinent
from 1526 to 1857. The
mausoleum's gateway features
breathtakingly intricate
mosaics, forming geometric
and epigraphic designs. One
of Asia's oldest continuously
inhabited cities, Samarkand
became the capital of the
Timurid Empire in 1370.
Timur set about regenerating
the cityscape with the help of
thousands of craftspeople.

Darvaza crater, Turkmenistan

In 1971, Soviet engineers were drilling for oil here when they hit a natural gas pocket. The ground beneath their drilling rig collapsed, leaving a 69-m (226-ft) wide crater. The engineers were concerned about releasing poisonous gases into nearby towns, so they decided to burn the gas off, thinking it might take a few weeks. The crater has been burning ever since.

FAR LEFT:

Göreme National Park, Cappadocia, Turkey
This region is known for its many tall spires of volcanic tuff, known as 'fairy chimneys'. They were formed as a soft layer of tuff was eroded, with caps of harder basalt protecting the spires beneath. Around the town of Göreme, some of the fairy chimneys were carved out into dwellings and places of worship over the centuries, many of them in use today as hotels and restaurants.

LEFT:

Mount Nemrut, Adiyaman, Turkey
The summit of Mount Nemrut is the location of the 1st-century BC tomb-sanctuary of King Antiochus I Theos of Commagene. Surrounding the tomb were 8–9-m (26–30-ft) high statues of himself, animals and gods from the ancient Greek, Armenian and Medes pantheons. At some point, the heads of all the statues were removed from their bodies and many have received damage to their noses. The pictured statue may depict the head of Apollo–Mithras.

Lut Desert, Iran
Dasht-e Lut records the world's hottest land surface temperatures, reaching 70.7°C (159.3°F). This desert of rock, sand and salt flats covers 51,800 sq km (20,000 sq miles). It is known for its *kalouts*, sometimes called 'sand castles', which are yardangs sculpted by the erosion of wind-blown sand.

Tachara, Persepolis, Iran
From c. 550 to 330 BC, the great complex at Persepolis was the ceremonial capital of the Achaemenid Empire, which stretched from Greece and Libya in the west to Pakistan in the east. Archeologists believe that Persepolis, which boasted palaces, temples, military quarters, imposing gateways and monumental staircases, was inhabited only seasonally. The Tachara (pictured at far right) was a palace building located on a great terrace. It features many fine bas-reliefs, including that of guards (pictured right) and servants bringing gifts (far right) on the nearby staircase.

ABOVE:

Ajanta Caves, Maharashtra, India

These 30 caves, cut into the cliffs from the 2nd century BC to around 480 AD, are home to some of the world's finest Buddhist art, from extraordinarily detailed and expressive paintings to rock-cut sculptures. The caves served as monasteries, resting places for pilgrims and halls of worship.

RIGHT:

Cave 26, Ajanta Caves

This worship hall, created in the late 5th century AD, has side aisles created by rows of columns patterned with foliage. The many elaborate sculptures include a depiction of the demon Mara's daughters attempting to seduce the Buddha. The central stupa features a seated Buddha.

Taj Mahal, Agra, India

The Taj Mahal was commissioned in 1632 by the Mughal emperor Shah Jahan as a mausoleum for his favourite wife, Mumtaz Mahal, who died while giving birth to their 14th child. The monument was inspired by Persian and earlier Mughal architecture, including Samarkand's Gur-e Amir. During construction, which lasted 21 years, 1000 elephants hauled the marble blocks from quarries 360km (220 miles) away. Since human forms are prohibited in Islamic architecture, the arched front portal (pictured right) features calligraphic and floral designs.

ABOVE AND ABOVE RIGHT:

Chittor Fort, Rajasthan, India
Chittor Fort was the capital of the Mewar Kingdom from the
7th century, changing hands many times over the centuries
before its Rajput inhabitants were overrun by the Mughals
in 1568. The walled citadel contains four palace complexes
(including the Rana Kumbha, pictured above right) and 19
temples, the majority of them Hindu but some Jain (such as the
Sathis Deori, pictured above).

OPPOSITE:

Kandariya Mahadeva, Khajuraho, Madhya Pradesh, India
The Kandariya Mahadeva is the largest of the Hindu temples
in the Khajuraho temple complex, which features 25 surviving
Hindu, Buddhist and Jain temples dating from the 9th
to 12th centuries. Like the other temples here, Kandariya
Mahadeva, constructed in around 1030, is famous for its
many erotic carvings depicting human couples and groups
in *maithuna* (coitus).

OPPOSITE:
**Humayun's Tomb,
Delhi, India**
The tomb of the Mughal
emperor Humayun was
designed in Persian style
in 1569–70. Like the later
Taj Mahal, it was inspired
by Timur's mausoleum in
Samarkand (see page 179).
The tomb is at the centre of a
Char Bargh, a Persian garden
with a quadrilateral layout
representing the four gardens
of Paradise.

RIGHT:
**Diwan-i-Am,
Red Fort, Delhi**
The Red Fort was constructed
by the Mughal emperor Shah
Jahan in 1639 and remained
the main residence of the
Mughal dynasty until 1856.
The fort gets its name from
its protective walls of red
sandstone. The Diwan-i-Am,
with its elegant engraved
arches, was Shah Jahan's
audience chamber.

The Pacific

Encompassing Australasia, Melanesia, Micronesia and Polynesia, as well as the outlying Pacific islands of the Galápagos and Philippines, this region takes a share of its character from the vast ocean, its islands' staggeringly beautiful landforms and the determined spirit of its peoples. Polynesia was the last major region of the world (barring Antarctica) to be settled, by Austronesian peoples travelling by canoe. New Zealand came last of all, in 1250 to 1300 AD, when eastern Polynesians came ashore, establishing the Maori culture. We can see the unique monuments of these island cultures in the *moai* of Easter Island and the political and spiritual centres of Nan Madol and Taputapuatea.

Many of the natural wonders of this region were created by the Ring of Fire, the arc of volcanism and violent plate movements that bounds the western, northern and eastern Pacific Ocean. The Ring is responsible for the geothermal activity of New Zealand's North Island and the volcanoes of the Philippines, but is not implicated in the formation of the Hawaiian or Galápagos Islands, which were born over hotspots in the mantle. Australia, inhabited by Aboriginal peoples for 50,000 years, is the largest landmass in this region and by far the biggest economy. Here we find one of the world's most iconic buildings, Sydney Opera House, as well as land- and seascapes that awe with their scale and wildness.

OPPOSITE:
Great Barrier Reef, Australia
The world's largest coral reef system stretches for over 2300km (1400 miles) in the Coral Sea, off the coast of Queensland. The reef is built from the exoskeletons of billions of living organisms called coral polyps. The structure supports extraordinary biodiversity, including 2195 plant species, 5000 molluscs, 1500 fish, 400 corals, 215 birds, 30 cetaceans and six sea turtles.

LEFT:

**Blue Mountains,
New South Wales, Australia**
The valleys of the Blue
Mountains have been
inhabited by the Darak
and Gundangara for
around 40,000 years. For
the Gundangara, this
region was home to the
mythical sisters Meehni,
Wimlah and Gunnedoo.
The Blue Mountains are a
range of peaks and plateau
escarpments that form part
of the 3500-km (2175-mile)
Great Dividing Range.

RIGHT:

**Hanging Rock,
Blue Mountains**
The sandstone spire
of Hanging Rock juts
precariously over the Grose
Valley. Many different species
of eucalyptus dominate
the valley, from *Eucalyptus
sieberi* above 800m (2600ft) to
Eucalyptus oblonga at lower
altitudes. The Grose River
is known for its platypuses,
which are the animal emblem
of New South Wales.

Uluru, Northern Territory, Australia

Also known as Ayers Rock, in honour of the late 19th-century Chief Secretary of South Australia, Sir Henry Ayers, Uluru is a 348-m (1142-ft) high sandstone formation. The rock is sacred to the Pitjantjatjara Anangu, who prefer that visitors do not climb it, partly from concern about their safety. Uluru is an inselberg, or island mountain, which has escaped erosion because of its remarkable lack of jointing.

Sydney Opera House, New South Wales, Australia
Designed by Danish architect Jørn Utzon, this iconic performing arts centre was completed in 1973. The building is in Expressionist style, eschewing conventional forms to achieve a visionary and emotionally engaging masterpiece. The 'shells' of the roof are made from precast concrete, covered by 1,056,006 tiles in glossy white and matte cream.

Milford Sound, South Island, New Zealand

Milford Sound is one of 15 fjords in Fjordland National Park, all carved during past ice ages. According to Maori myth, the hero Tu-te-raki-whanoa carved the fjords with his adze Te Hamo. The sound is lined by a fjord's typically steep rock faces and peaks, including Mitre Peak (centre), 1683m (5522ft) tall, named by the British in the mid-19th century for its resemblance to a bishop's mitre.

Lady Knox Geyser, Waiotapu, North Island, New Zealand

The Reporoa Caldera, part of the Taupo Volcanic Zone, is responsible for the geothermal activity at Waiotapu, including geysers, bubbling mud pools and hot springs. The Lady Knox Geyser was named in the early 20th century after the daughter of the 15th governor of New Zealand. The geyser is made to erupt every day, the jet reaching 20m (66ft) high, by pouring a soapy surfactant into the vent.

Champagne Pool, Waiotapu

This hot spring gets its name from its bubbles of carbon dioxide. The water at the bottom of the pool reaches 260°C (500°F), but at the surface it is a steady 75°C (167°F). The orange deposits around the edges of the spring are crystals of the arsenic sulphide minerals orpiment and realgar.

Diamond Head, O'ahu, Hawaiian Islands
Diamond Head is a volcanic cone formed by an eruption of the the Ko'olau Volcano about 400,000–500,000 years ago. Ko'olau is one of the 17 major volcanoes that make up the Hawaiian Islands and formed over a hotspot in the mantle under the Pacific Plate. The movement of the plate created a long volcanic chain, starting in Hawaii and ending at the Aleutian Trench.

Kilauea, Hawaii
The active volcano Kilauea, only 300,000–600,000 years old, is the second youngest product of the Hawaiian hotspot: the Loihi Seamount, an active submarine volcano about 35km (22 miles) off the southeast coast of the island of Hawaii, is the youngest. Kilauea, which emerged above sea level around 100,000 years ago, has been erupting almost continuously since 1983.

Moai, Easter Island
Between around 1250 AD and 1500, the inhabitants of Easter Island carved blocks of tuff and other local rocks into more than 900 giant human figures, called *moai*. These statues are believed to represent the sculptors' deified ancestors, many of them positioned on platforms around the island's perimeter, facing inland towards their family lands. Although the *maoi* are whole-body statues, they are often mistakenly called 'heads' because their heads are disproportionately large and some statues are buried up to their shoulders. The more recent *moai* had *pukao*, or chieftain's topknots, on their heads, carved from a lightweight red scoria.

Nan Madol, Pohnpei, Micronesia

Located just off the small island of Temwen, Nan Madol was the capital of the Saudeleur Dynasty, which ruled Pohnpei and its surrounding islands from around 1100 to 1628 AD. The city was built in a lagoon on around 100 small artificial islands, platforms of stone and coral, linked by canals. The complex is surrounded by walls made of stacked basalt columns. It is believed that Nan Madol was home to the dynasty's rulers and priests, as well as the chiefs of rival families, who were required to live there so they could be monitored. All food and fresh water was brought to Nan Madol by boat.

**Chocolate Hills,
Bohol, Philippines**
Over an area of 50 sq km
(20 sq miles), the 'Chocolate
Hills' are more than 1260 low,
hump-like hills with grass that
turns brown, like chocolate,
in the dry season. They are a
geological feature known as
haycock hills, conical mounds
of limestone that were eroded
into their current shape by
rivers and rainfall. Local
legend tells that the hills were
formed by two fighting giants,
who threw sand, mud and
boulders at each other.

BELOW:

Mount Mayon, Luzon, Philippines

This active stratovolcano is renowned for its perfectly symmetrical cone shape, formed from layers of basaltic-andesitic lava. Mayon is part of the Ring of Fire, the horseshoe-shaped region around the edges of the Pacific, Nazca and Cocos plates, among others, where there are 425 volcanoes and 90 per cent of the world's earthquakes take place. Mayon has erupted more than 47 times in the last 500 years.

RIGHT:

Rice Terraces of Ifugao, Luzon, Philippines

At least 1000 years old, these terraces were carved into the mountains of Ifugao for the cultivation of taro, which was replaced by rice in around 1600. The terraces are shored up by mud and stone walls and watered by an irrigation system that channels water from the forest above. A deep understanding of local hydrology and climate allows Ifugao farmers to grow crops at over 1000m (3280ft) above sea level.

LEFT:

Puerto Princesa Subterranean River, Palawan, Philippines

One of the longest known underground rivers in the world, this subterranean section of the Cabayugan River is 8.2km (5.1 miles) long and is navigable by boat 4.3km (2.7 miles) from the entrance on the West Philippine Sea. The limestone cave system features nine species of bats, whip spiders, waterfalls and several large chambers, including the 360-m (1180-ft) long Italian's Chamber.

RIGHT:

Marae Taputapuatea, Raiatea, French Polynesia

A *marae* is a large sacred space for religious or social ceremonies. There are several *marae* in the 1000-year-old complex at Taputapuatea, which probably had different functions, some political and some sacrificial. It is believed that chiefs and priests from all over eastern Polynesia would gather here, voyaging by outrigger canoe.

Volcán Alcedo giant tortoise, Isabela, Galápagos Islands

This giant tortoise lives only on the caldera and slopes of the Alcedo volcano, on Isabela, the largest of the Galápagos Islands. This species is one of 11 surviving species of giant tortoises endemic to the different islands and volcanoes of the Galápagos Islands. The largest living species of tortoises, they are also among the longest-lived vertebrates, with wild lifespans of over 100 years. Neck length and shell size and shape differ between the species, depending on the climate and flora of their distinct habitat. Charles Darwin's observations of these differences in 1835 helped him to develop his theory of evolution.

Bartolomé, Galápagos Islands

Named after Darwin's shipmate Sir Bartholomew James Sullivan, this volcanic islet is one of the younger islands in the archipelago. The archipelago was formed by the Galápagos hotspot, starting at least 8 million years ago and continuing to the present. Although Bartolomé is uninhabited, the archipelago is home to 25,000 Ecuadorian citizens. Bartolomé itself is home to the Galápagos penguin, the only penguin species to live on the equator.

Rock Islands, Palau

There are between 250 and 300 Rock Islands in Palau's Southern Lagoon, the remnants of ancient coral reefs that have been uplifted by volcanism. Many of the islands have a mushroom-like shape, narrower at the tide line than above it. This is caused by the constant erosion of breaking waves. Nearly all the islands are uninhabited, but they are popular tourist destinations because of their perfect diving conditions and diverse marine life, including 385 coral species.

Picture Credits